Nursery Rhymes and Songs.

By Richard Carlin.
Illustrated by Mark Weinstein.

Amsco Publications
New York/London/Sydney

Cover art direction by Mike Bell (UK)
Cover illustration by Graham Percy (UK)
Text illustrations by Marc Chase Weinstein (USA)
Piano arrangements by Richard Lane (USA)

Order No. AM 60211
US International Standard Book Number: 0.8256.2443.6
UK International Standard Book Number: 0.7119.0720.X

Exclusive Distributors:
Music Sales Corporation
257 Park Avenue South, New York, NY 10010 USA
Music Sales Limited
8/9 Frith Street, London W1V 5TZ England
Music Sales Pty. Limited
120 Rothschild Street, Rosebery, Sydney, NSW 2018, Australia

Printed in the United States of America by
Vicks Lithograph and Printing Corporation

The Ants Came Marching

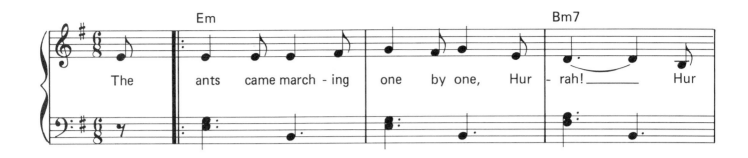

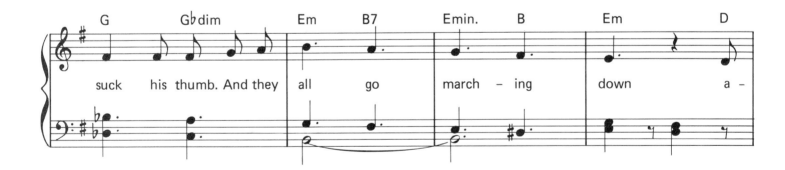

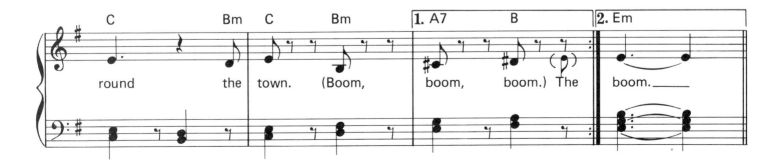

The ants came marching two by two, Hurrah! Hurrah!
The ants came marching two by two
The little one stopped to tie his shoe.
They all go marching down around the town.
(Boom, boom, boom.)

The ants came marching three by three . . .
The little one stopped to climb a tree.

The ants came marching four by four . . .
The little one stopped to shut the door . . .

The ants came marching five by five . . .
The little one stopped to take a dive . . .

The ants came marching six by six . . .
The little one stopped to pick up sticks . . .

The ants came marching seven by seven . . .
The little one stopped to go to heaven . . .

The ants came marching eight by eight . . .
The little one stopped to shut the gate . . .

The ants came marching nine by nine . . .
The little one stopped to scratch his spine.

The ants came marching ten by ten . . .
The little one stopped to say   *The end.*

Baa! Baa! Black Sheep

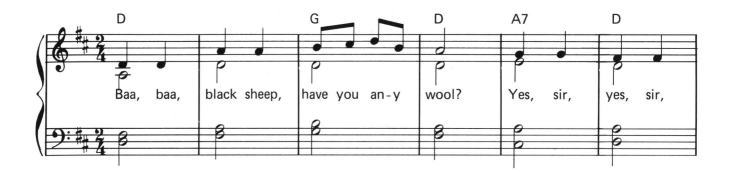

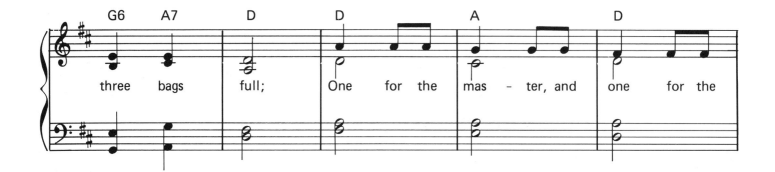

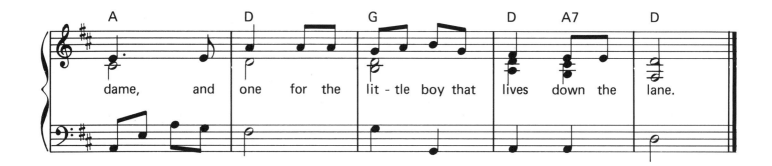

Ding Dong Bell

Ding dong bell! Pus-sy's in the well! Who put her in?

Lit-tle Tom-my Green. Who pulled her out? Lit-tle Tom-my Stout. What a

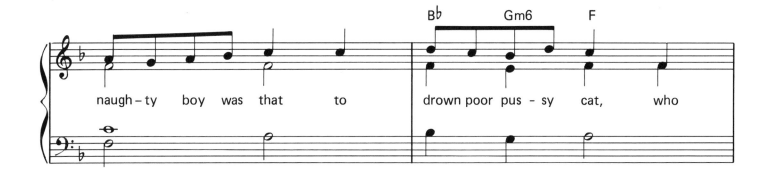

naugh-ty boy was that to drown poor pus-sy cat, who

ne'er did an-y harm, but killed all the mice in his fa-ther's barn.

The Farmer In The Dell

The farm – er in the dell, the farm – er in the dell,

hi – ho the mer – ry oh, the farm – er in the dell.

2 – The farmer takes a wife
3 – The wife takes a child
4 – The child takes a dog
5 – The dog takes a bone

Fiddle-De-Dee

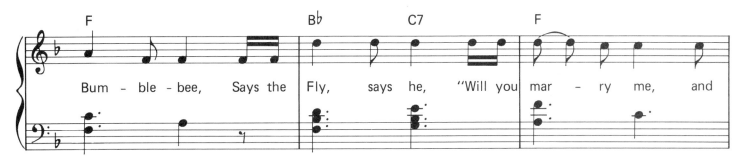

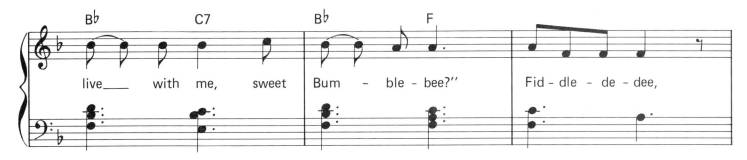

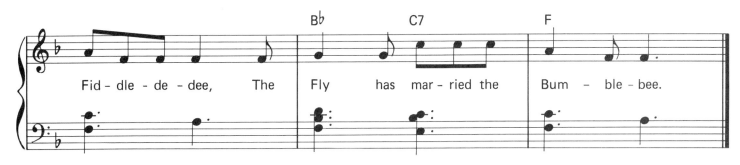

Fiddle - de - dee, fiddle - de - dee,
The Fly has married the Bumblebee.
Says the Fly, says he, "Will you marry me
And live with me, sweet Bumblebee?"
Fiddle - de - dee, fiddle - de - dee,
The Fly has married the Bumblebee.

Fiddle - de - dee, etc.
Says the Bee, says she, "I'll live under your wing,
And you'll never know I carry a sting."
Fiddle - de - dee, etc.

Fiddle - de - dee, etc.
And when Parson Beetle had married the pair,
They both went out to take the air;
Fiddle - de - dee, etc.

Georgie Porgie

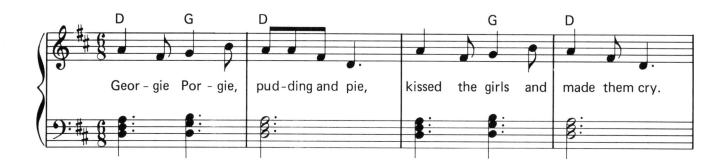

Geor - gie Por - gie, pud-ding and pie, kissed the girls and made them cry.

When the boys came out to play, Geor - gie Por - gie ran a - way.

Here We Go Gathering Nuts in May

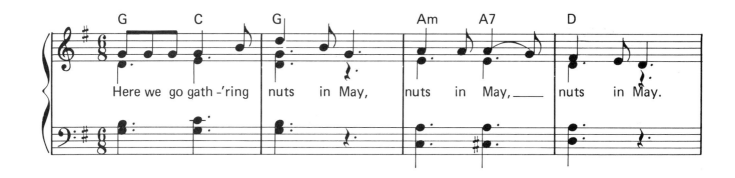

Have A Little Dog

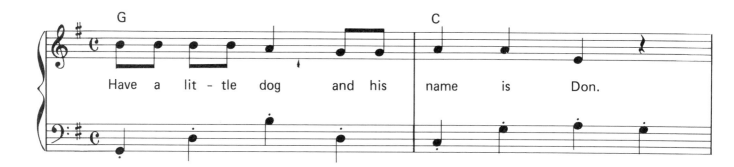

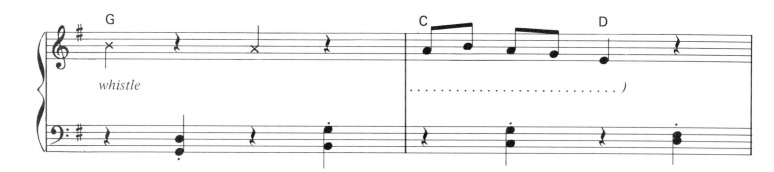

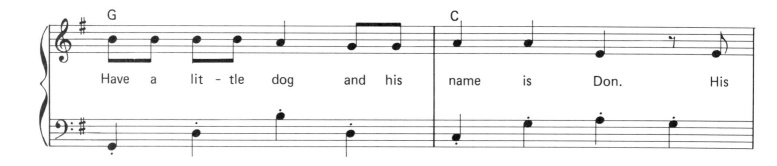

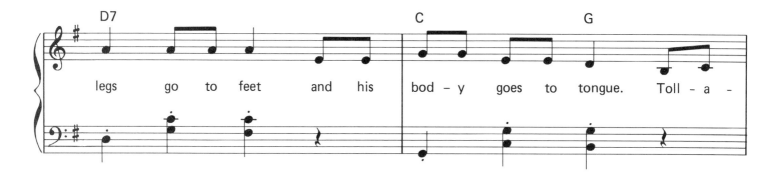

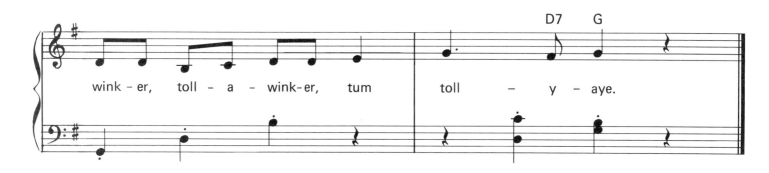

2. Have a little box about three feet square *(whistle)*
   Have a little box about three feet square,
   When I go to travel I put him in there,
   Toll - a - winker, toll - a - winker, tum tolly - aye.

3. When I go to travel I travel like an ox,
   And in my vest pocket I carry that box, etc.
   (whistle) (2 times)

4. Had a little hen and her color was fair,
   Sat her on a bomb and she hatched me a hare, etc.
   (whistle) (2 times)

5. The hare turned a horse about six feet high,
   If you want to beat this you'll have to tell a lie, etc.
   (whistle) (2 times)

6. I had a little mule and his name was Jack.
   I rode him on his tail to save his back.
   (whistle) (2 times)

7. I had a little mule and his name was Jay,
   I pulled his tail to hear him bray.
   (whistle) (2 times)

8. I had a little mule he was made of hay,
   First big wind come along and blowed him away.
   (whistle) (2 times)

Hey Diddle Diddle

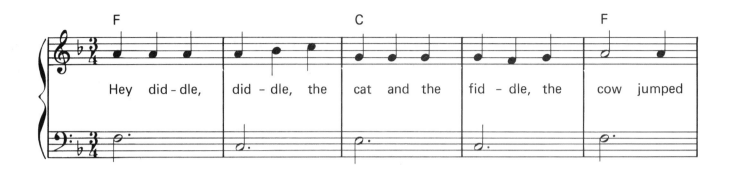

Hey did-dle, did-dle, the cat and the fid-dle, the cow jumped

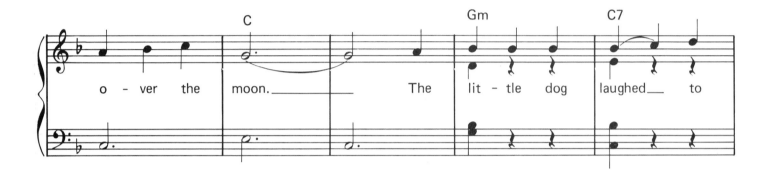

o-ver the moon. The lit-tle dog laughed to

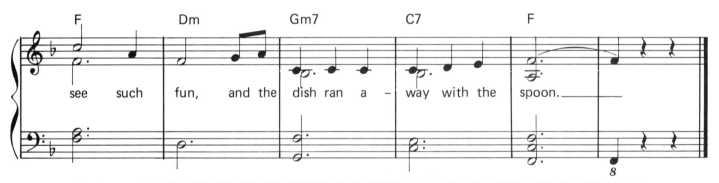

see such fun, and the dish ran a-way with the spoon.

Hickory Dickory Dock

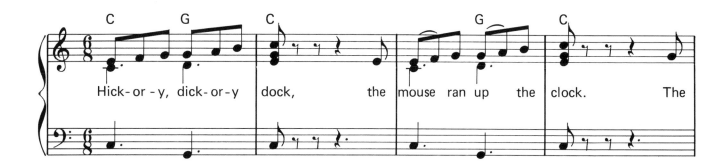

Hick-or-y, dick-or-y dock, the mouse ran up the clock. The

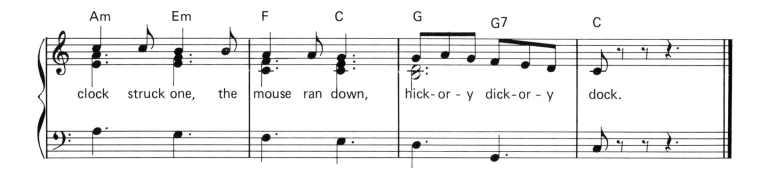

clock struck one, the mouse ran down, hick-or-y dick-or-y dock.

Humpty Dumpty

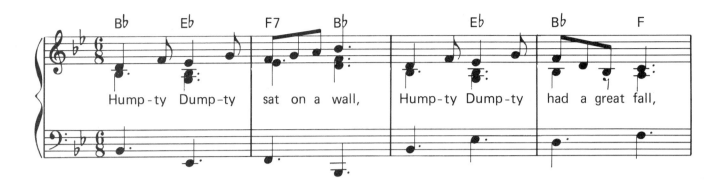

Hump-ty Dump-ty sat on a wall, Hump-ty Dump-ty had a great fall,

all the King's hors-es and all the King's men, could-n't put Hump-ty to - geth-er a-gain.

Hush, Little Baby

Hush little baby don't say a word,
Mama's gonna buy you a mockin' - bird.

If that mockin' - bird don't sing,
Papa's gonna buy you a diamond ring.

If that ring is made of brass,
Mama's gonna buy you a lookin' glass.

If that lookin' glass gets broke,
Papa's gonna buy you a billy goat.

If that billy goat don't pull,
Mama's gonna buy you a cart and bull.

If that cart and bull turn over,
Papa's gonna buy you a dog named Rover.

If that dog named Rover don't bark,
Mama's gonna buy you a horse and cart.

It that horse and cart fall down,
You'll be the sweetest little boy in town!

I Had A Little Rooster

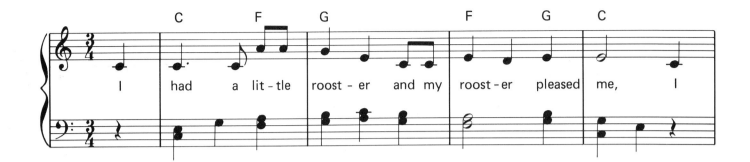

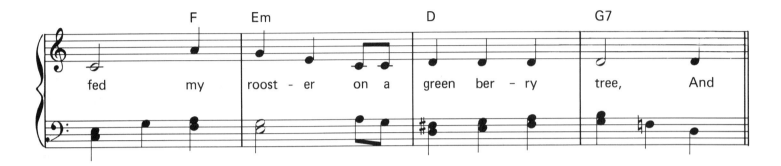

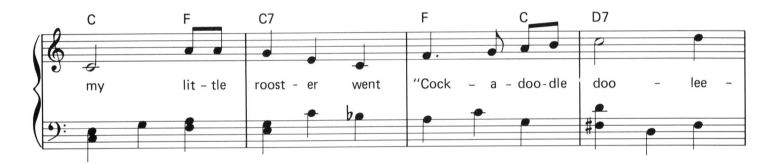

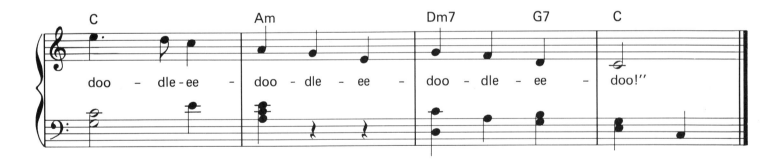

I had a little hen and my hen pleased me,
I fed my hen on a green berry tree,
And my little hen went "Cluck! Cluck! Cluck!"
And my little rooster went "Cock - a - doodle - doo - lee —
Doodle - ee - doodle - ee - doodle - ee - doo!"

I had a little duck, *(etc.)*
I fed my duck, *(etc.)*
And my little duck went "Quack! Quack! Quack!"
And my little hen went. *(etc.)*

I Saw Three Ships

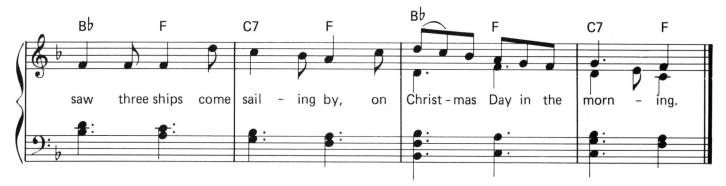

I saw three ships come sail-ing by, on Christ-mas Day, on Christ-mas Day. I

saw three ships come sail-ing by, on Christ-mas Day in the morn-ing.

I'm A Little Teapot

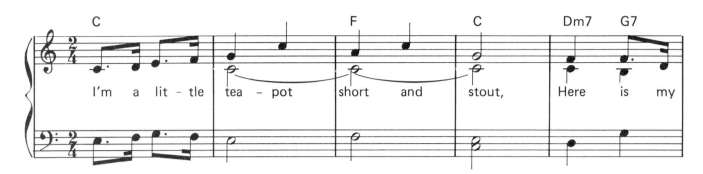

I'm a lit – tle tea – pot short and stout, Here is my

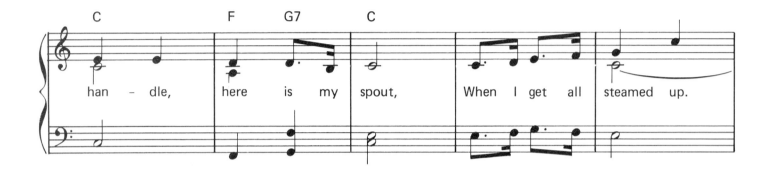

han – dle, here is my spout, When I get all steamed up.

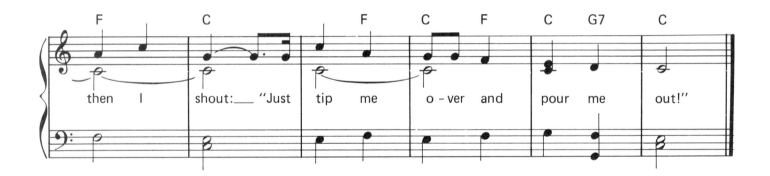

then I shout:___ "Just tip me o - ver and pour me out!"

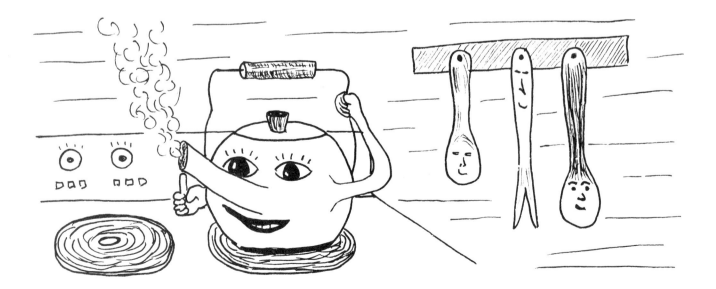

Jack And Jill

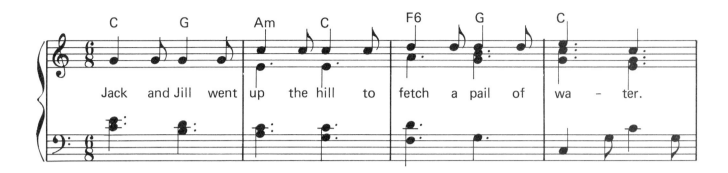

Jack and Jill went up the hill to fetch a pail of wa — ter.

Jack fell down, and broke his crown, and Jill came tumb – ling af — ter.

Lazy Katy, Will You Get Up?

Lazy Katy, will you get up,
You get up, you get up?
Lazy Katy, will you get up
This cold and frosty morning?

No, Mother, I won't get up,
Won't get up, won't get up.
No, Mother, I won't get up
This cold and frosty morning.

What if I give you some bread and jam,
Bread and jam, bread and jam?
What if I give you some bread and jam
This cold and frosty morning?

No, Mother, I won't get up . . .

What if I give you some bacon and egg,
Bacon and egg, bacon and egg . . .

No, Mother, I won't get up . . .

What if I give you a crack on the head,
Crack on the head, crack on the head . . .

Yes, Mother, I will get up,
Will get up, will get up.
Yes, Mother, I will get up
This cold and frosty morning.

Little Bo-Peep

Lit-tle Bo-peep has lost her sheep, and does-n't know where to find them.

Leave them a-lone, and they'll come home, bring-ing their tails be-hind them.

Little Bird, Little Bird

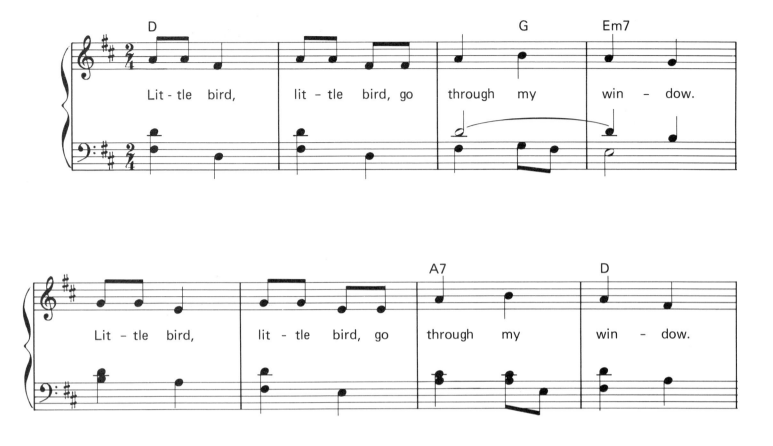

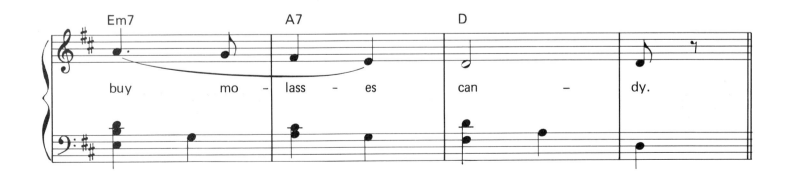

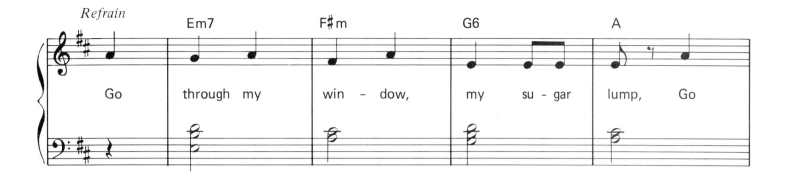

Refrain

Go through my win - dow, my su - gar lump, Go

through my win - dow, my su - gar lump.

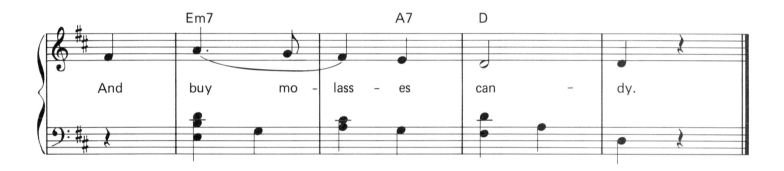

And buy mo - lass - es can - dy.

Blue bird, blue bird,
Fly through my window,
Blue bird, blue bird,
Fly through my window,
Blue bird, blue bird,
Fly through my window,
And buy molasses candy.

Refrain:

Fly through my window,
My little bird,
Fly through my window,
My little bird,
And buy molasses candy.

Little Boy Blue

Lit-tle Boy blue, come blow your horn, the sheep's in the mead-ow, the cow's in the corn.

Where's the boy who looks af-ter the sheep? He's un-der the hay-stack fast a-sleep.

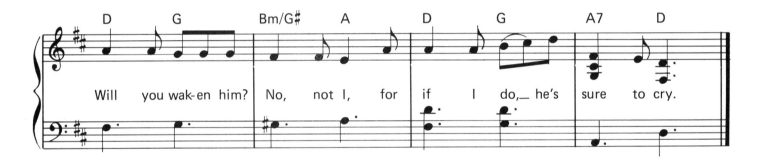

Will you wak-en him? No, not I, for if I do,— he's sure to cry.

Little Jack Horner

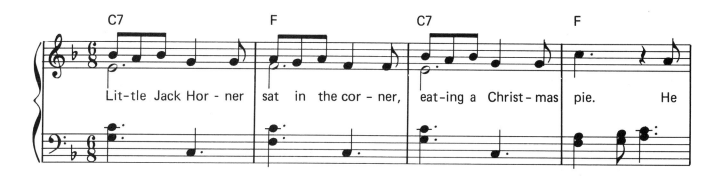

Mary Had A Little Lamb

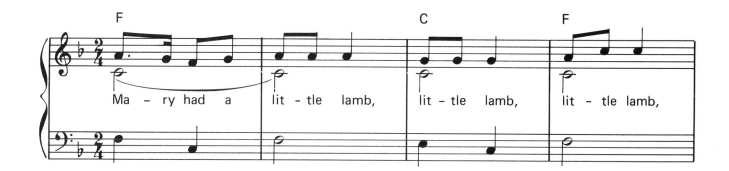

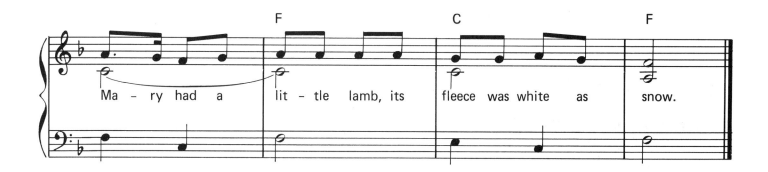

Little Tommy Tinker

Lit - tle Tom Tink – er   sat on a clink-er and   he be - gan to

cry:_____   'Ma!_____   Ma!_____   Poor lit - tle 'in -no-cent   I!"

London Bridge Is Falling Down

The Muffin Man

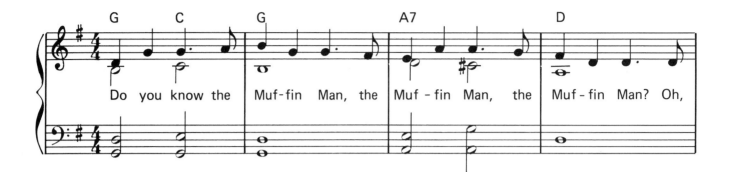

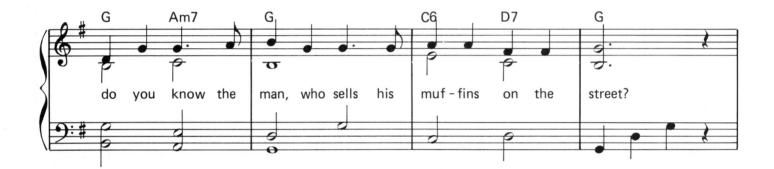

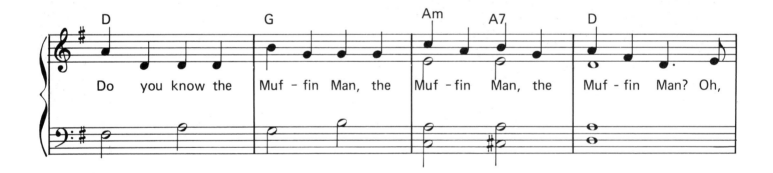

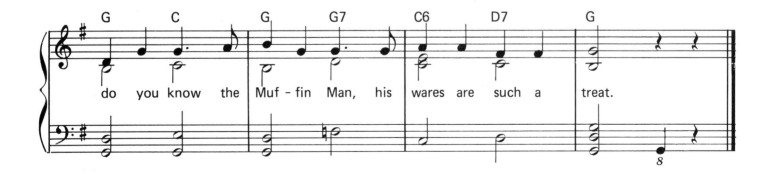

Now The Day Is Over

Now the day is o - ver night is draw-ing nigh,

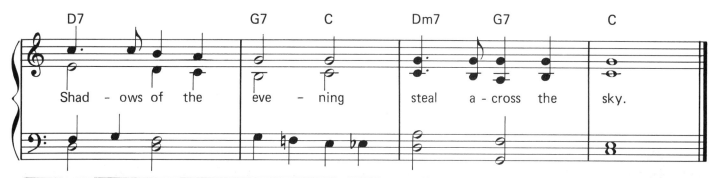

Shad - ows of the eve - ning steal a - cross the sky.

Oh Dear! What Can The Matter Be?

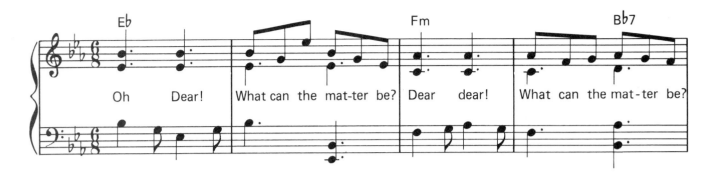

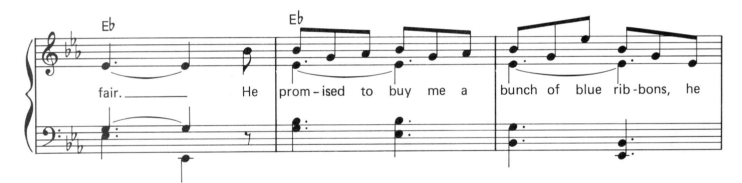

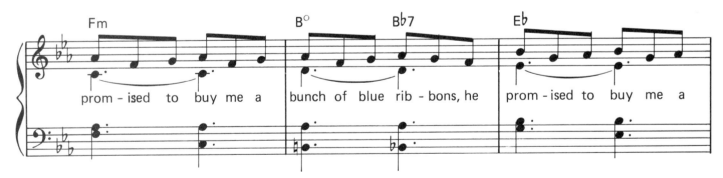

Oh Where Has My Little Dog Gone?

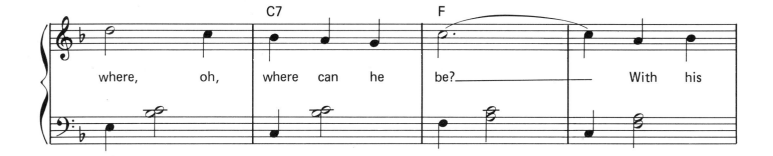

Oh, where, oh, where has my lit-tle dog gone? Oh,

where, oh, where can he be?_____ With his

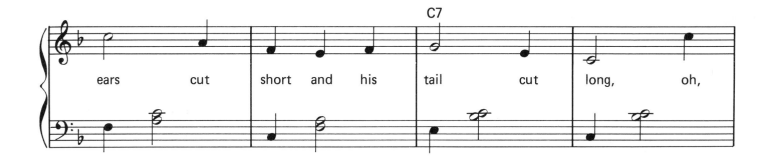

ears cut short and his tail cut long, oh,

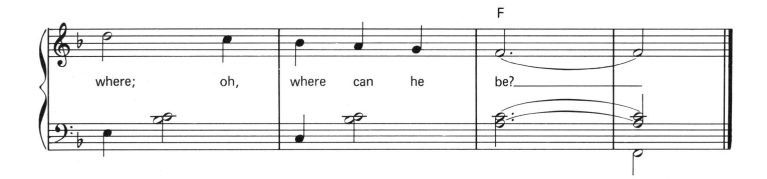

where; oh, where can he be?_____

Old Blue

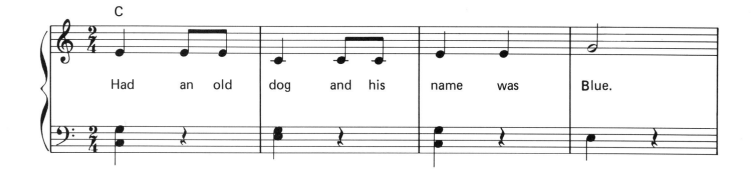

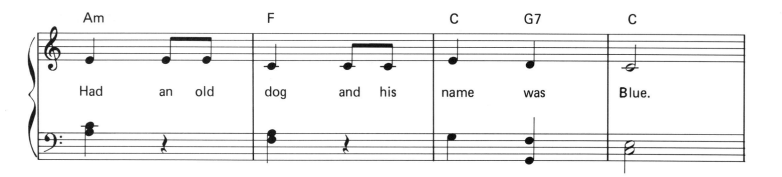

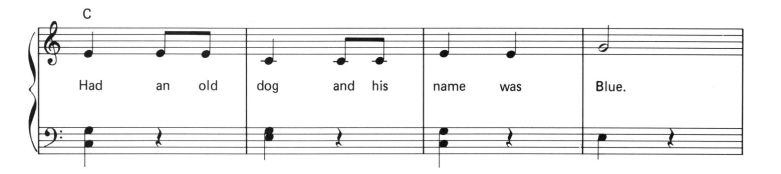

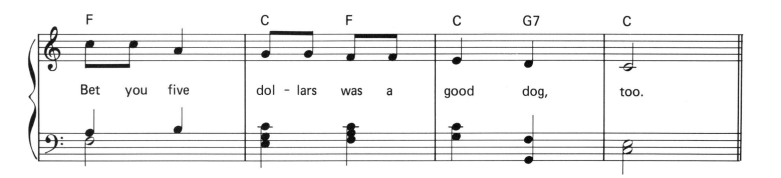

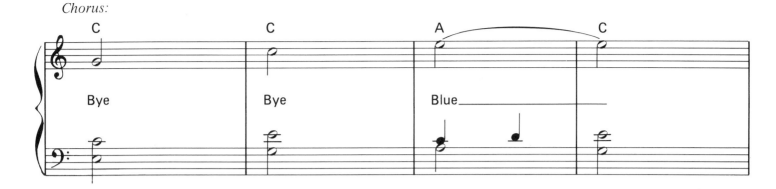

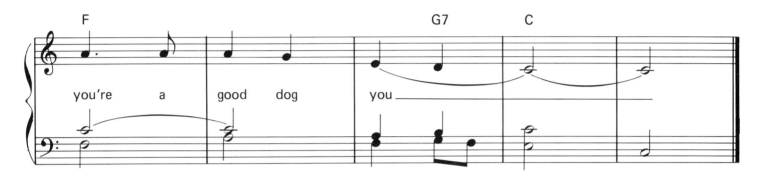

Everynight just about dark (3 times)
Blue goes out and begins to bark.
Chorus:

Everything just in a rush (3 times)
He treed a possum in a white-oak bush.
Chorus:

Possum walked out to the end of a limb (3 times)
Blue set down and talked to him.
Chorus:

Blue got sick and very sick (3 times)
Sent for the doctor to come here quick.
Chorus:

Doctor come and he come in a run (3 times)
Says "Old Blue, your hunting's done."
Chorus:

Blue he died and died so hard, (3 times)
Scratched little holes all around the yard.
Chorus:

Laid him out in a shady place (3 times)
Covered him o'er with a possum's face.
Chorus:

When I get to Heaven I'll tell you what I'll do (3 times)
I'll take my horn and blow for Blue.
Chorus:

Old Davey Jones

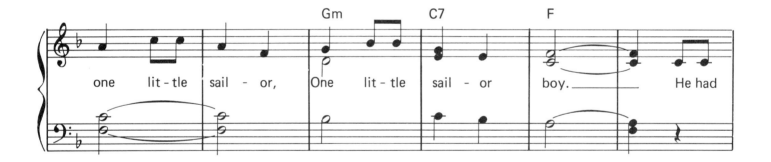

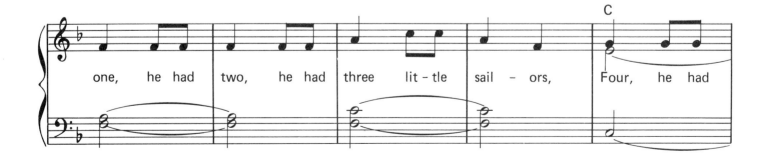

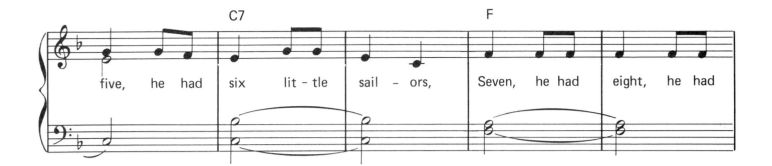

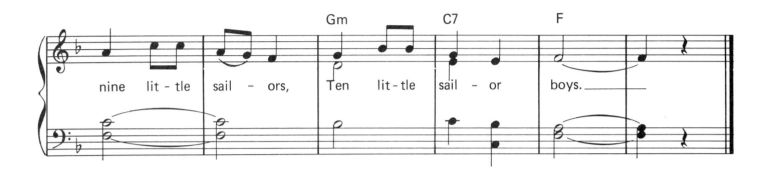

Old Davey Jones had one little sailor,
Old Davey Jones had one little sailor,
Old Davey Jones had one little sailor,
One little sailor boy.

He had one, he had two, he had three little sailors,
Four, he had five, he had six little sailors,
Seven, he had eight, he had nine little sailors,
Ten little sailor boys.

Old Davey Jones had ten little sailors . . .

He had ten, he had nine, he had eight little sailors,
Seven little, six little, five little sailors,
Four little, three little, two little sailors,
One little sailor boy.

Old King Cole

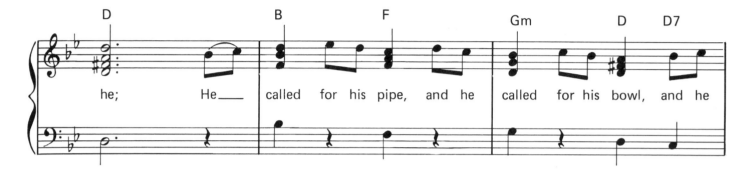

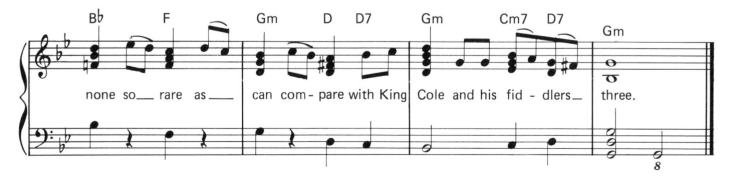

Old Mother Hubbard

Verse 1

Old Mother Hub-bard, she went to the cup-board, to fetch her poor dog a bone.

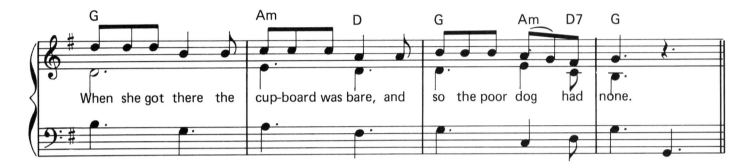

When she got there the cup-board was bare, and so the poor dog had none.

Verses 2 - 14

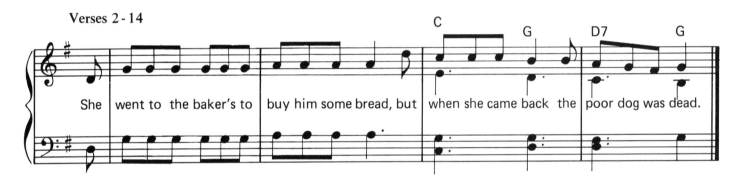

She went to the baker's to buy him some bread, but when she came back the poor dog was dead.

Extra Verses

She went to the undertaker's
To buy him a coffin;
But when she came back
The poor dog was laughing.

She took a clean dish,
To get him some tripe;
But when she came back
He was smoking a pipe.

She went to the fishmonger's
To buy him some fish;
But when she came back
He was licking the dish.

She went to the tavern
For white wine and red;
But when she came back
The dog stood on his head.

She went to the fruiterer's
To buy him some fruit;
But when she came back
He was playing the flute.

She went to the tailor's
To buy him a coat;
But when she came back
He was riding a goat.

She went to the hatter's
To buy him a hat;
But when she came back
He was feeding the cat.

She went to the barber's
To buy him a wig;
But when she came back
He was dancing a jig.

She went to the cobbler's
To buy him some shoes;
But when she came back
He was reading the news.

She went to the seamstress
To buy him some linen;
But when she came back
The dog was a - spinning.

She went to the hosier's
To buy him some hose;
But when she came back
He was dressed in his clothes.

The dame made a curtsey,
The dog made a bow;
The dame said, Your servant,
The dog said, Bow - wow.

One Finger, One Thumb, One Hand

One fin-ger, one thumb, one hand____ keep mov - ing,____ One

fin-ger, one thumb, one hand_ keep mov - ing,__ One fin-ger, one thumb, one hand,_ keep

mov - ing, And we'll all be hap - py and gay!

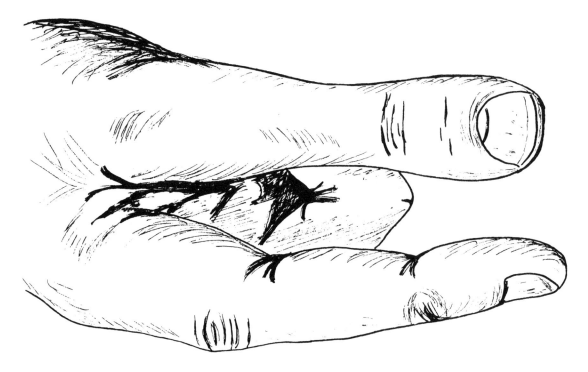

Pat-A-Cake, Pat-A-Cake, Baker's Man

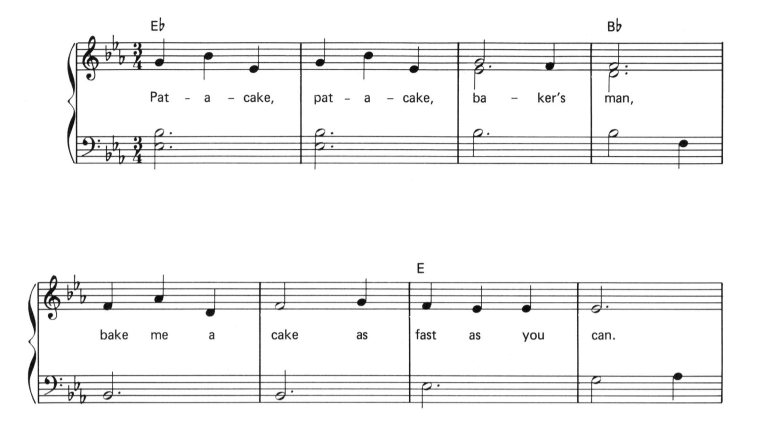

Pat - a - cake, pat - a - cake, ba - ker's man,

bake me a cake as fast as you can.

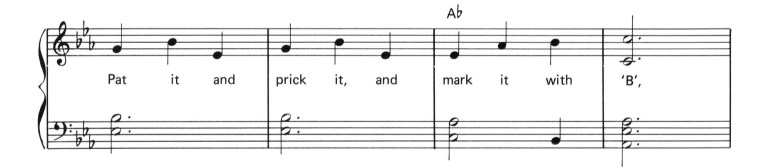

Pat it and prick it, and mark it with 'B',

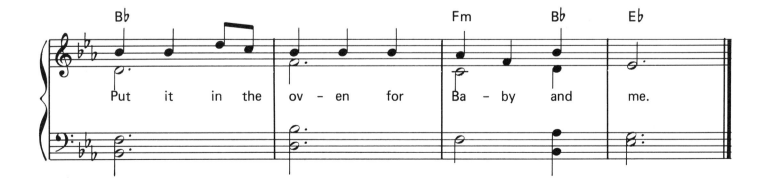

Put it in the ov - en for Ba - by and me.

Pat-A-Pan

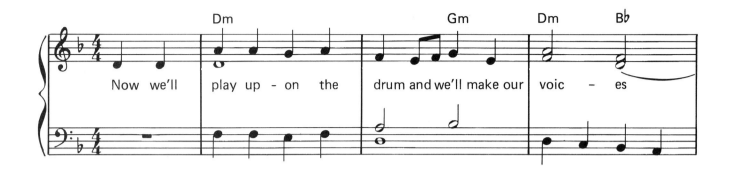

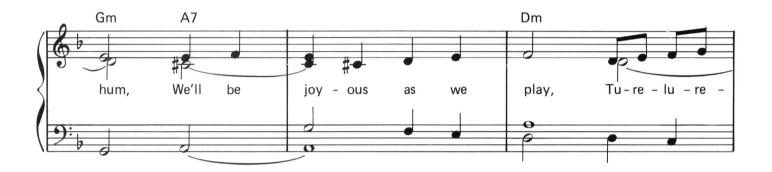

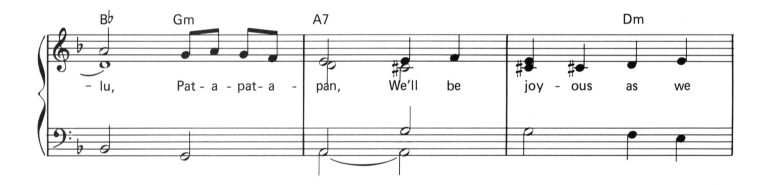

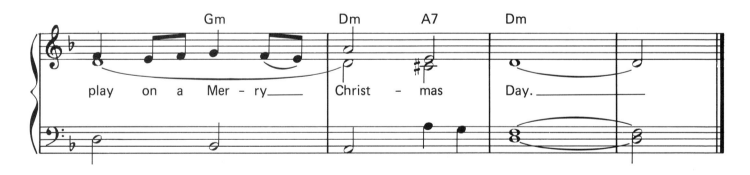

Now we'll play upon the drum and we'll make our voices hum,
We'll be joyous as we play, Tu - re - lu - re - lu, Pat - a - pat - a - pan,
We'll be joyous as we play on a Merry Christmas Day.
Just as men of other days raised their voices loud in praise, etc.
Brotherhood will rule and then peace on earth will come to men, etc.

Polly Put The Kettle On

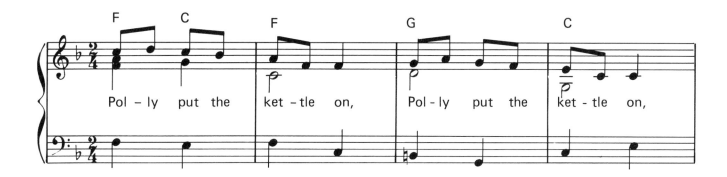

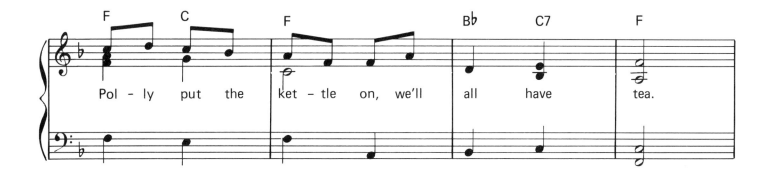

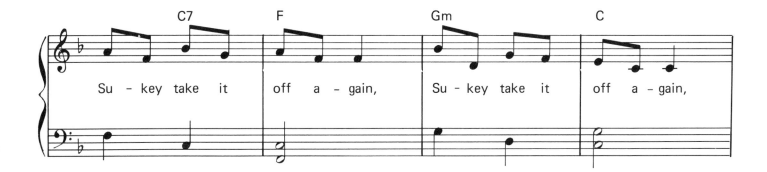

Pussy Cat, Pussy Cat

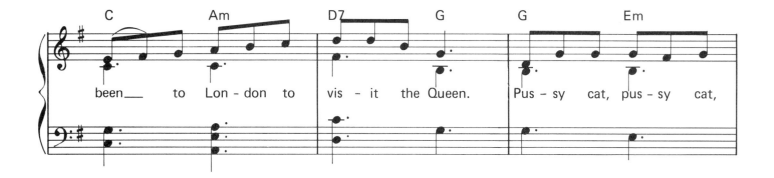

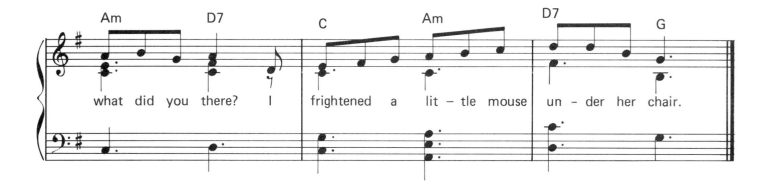

Ring-A-Ring O'Roses

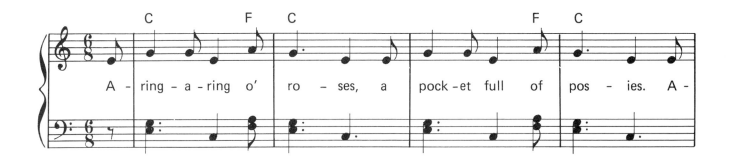

A - ring - a - ring o' ro — ses, a pock -et full of pos — ies. A -

tish — oo! A - tish — oo! We all fall down.

Row, Row, Row Your Boat

Row, row, row your boat, gent - ly down the stream,

mer - ri -ly, mer-ri - ly, mer - ri - ly, mer - ri - ly, life is but a dream.

Rock-A-Bye Baby

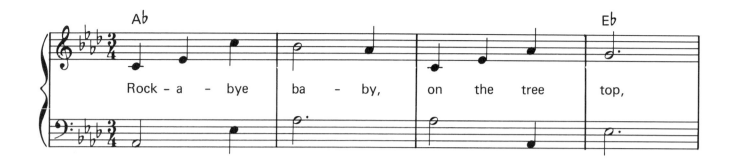

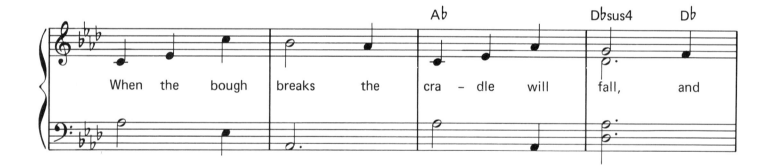

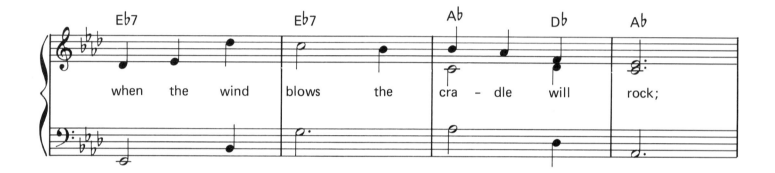

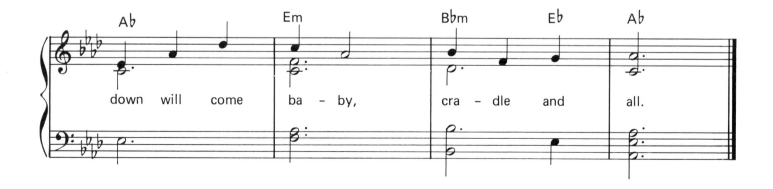

See-Saw, Margery Daw

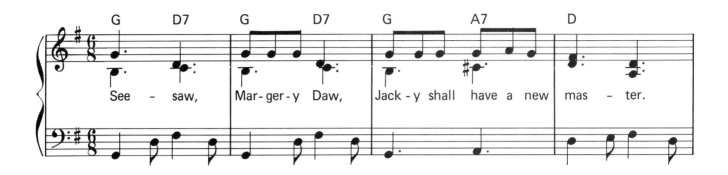

See - saw, Mar-ger-y Daw, Jack-y shall have a new mas - ter.

He shall have but a pen-ny a day, be - cause he can't work an-y fast – er.

Simple Simon

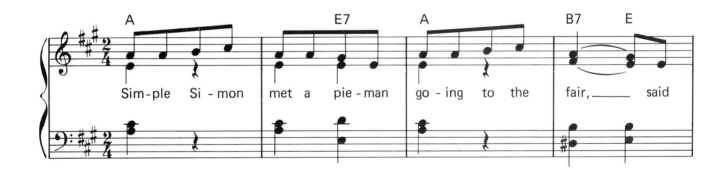

Sim-ple Si-mon met a pie-man go-ing to the fair,_____ said

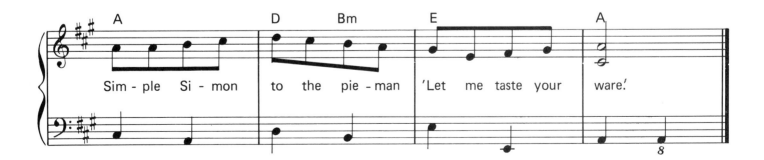

Sim - ple Si-mon to the pie-man 'Let me taste your ware.'

Short'nin' Bread

48

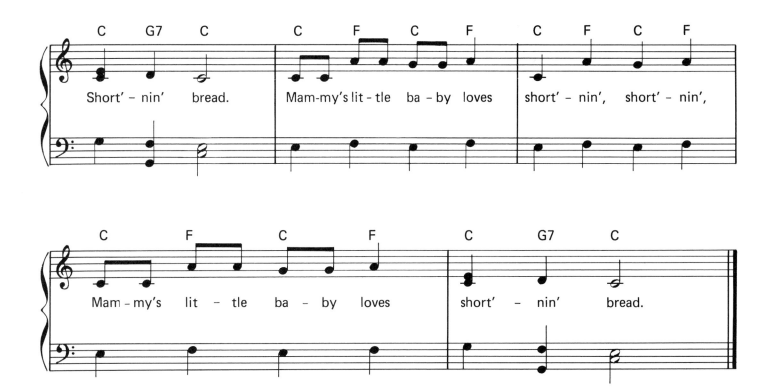

Three little children lyin' in bed;
Two were sick and the other' most dead!
Sent for the doctor; the doctor said,
"Feed those children on short' nin' bread."

Mammy's little baby loves short' nin', short' nin',
Mammy's little baby loves short' nin' bread.
Mammy's little baby loves short' nin', short' nin',
Mammy's little baby loves short' nin' bread.

Put on the skillet, put on the lid,
Mammy's gonna bake a little short' nin' bread.
That ain't all she's gonna do,
Mammy's gonna make a little coffee, too.

Then the little child, sick in bed,
When he hear tell of short' nin' bread,
Popped up well, he dance an' sing,
He almos' cut the pigeon wing.

I slip to the kitchen, slip up the lid,
Filled mah pockets full of short' nin' bread;
Stole the skillet, stole the lid,
Stole the gal making short' nin' bread.

They caught me with the skillet, they caught me
with the lid,
They caught me with the gal making short' nin' bread;
Paid for the skillet, paid for the lid,
Spent six months in jail, eatin' short' nin' bread.

Ten Little Indians

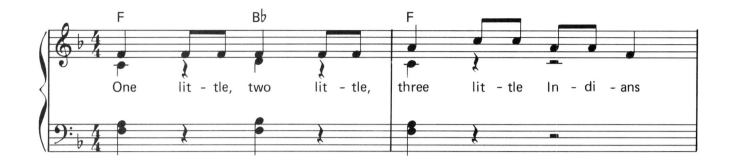

One lit - tle, two lit - tle, three lit - tle In - di - ans

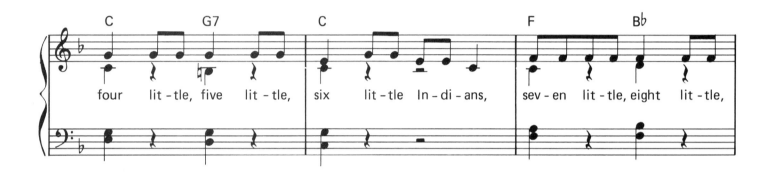

four lit - tle, five lit - tle, six lit - tle In - di - ans,

seven - en lit - tle, eight lit - tle,

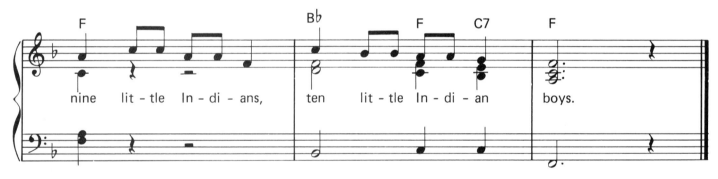

nine lit - tle In - di - ans, ten lit - tle In - di - an boys.

There Was A Crooked Man

There was a crook-ed man, and he walked a crook-ed mile, he found a crook-ed six – pence a – gainst a crook-ed stile. He bought a crook-ed cat, which caught a crook-ed mouse, and they all lived to-geth-er in a crook-ed lit – tle house.

There Was An Old Woman Who Lived In A Shoe

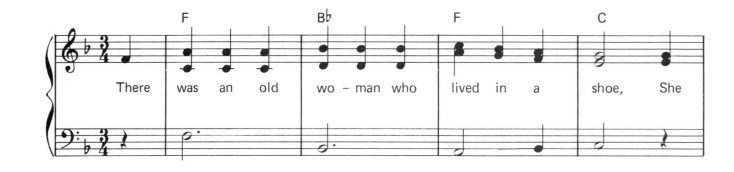

There was an old wo – man who lived in a shoe, She

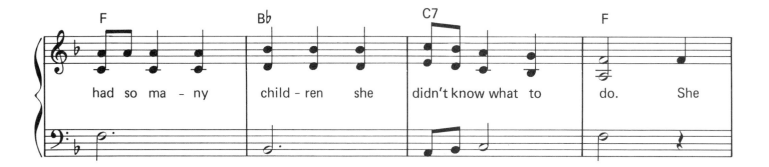

had so ma – ny child – ren she didn't know what to do. She

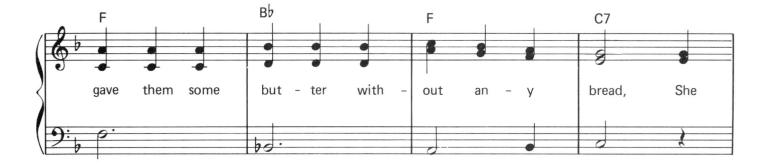

gave them some but – ter with – out an – y bread, She

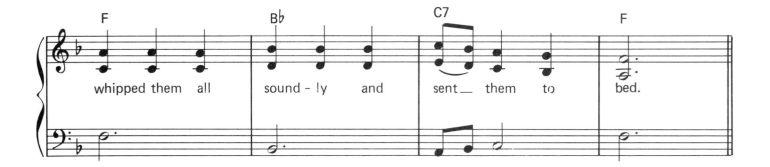

whipped them all sound – ly and sent__ them to bed.

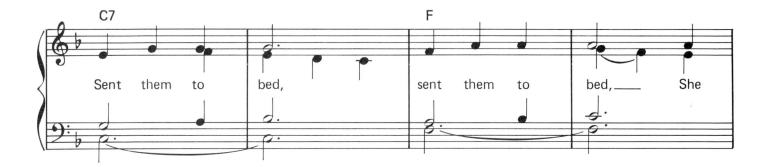

Sent them to bed, sent them to bed, ___ She

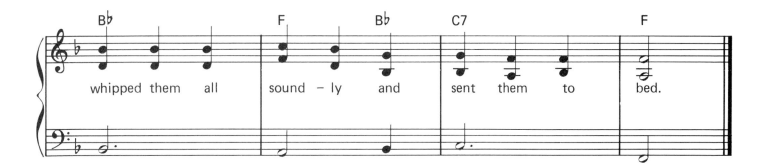

whipped them all sound-ly and sent them to bed.

There was an old woman who lived in a shoe
She had so many children she didn't know what to do.
She gave them some butter without any bread,
She whipped them all soundly and sent them to bed.
Sent them to bed, sent them to bed,
She whipped them all soundly and sent them to bed.

Then all those poor children crept under the clothes,
The cold pinched their fingers and also their toes,
And eating their butter without any bread,
Was not very nice for supper, they said.
Supper they said, supper they said,
Was not very nice for supper, they said.

And then the old woman who lived in the shoe,
She felt so very sorry she didn't know what to do,
She ran to the baker's to get them some bread,
And kissed them all sweetly and then they were fed.
Then they were fed, then they were fed,
She kissed them all sweetly and then they were fed.

There Were Ten In A Bed!

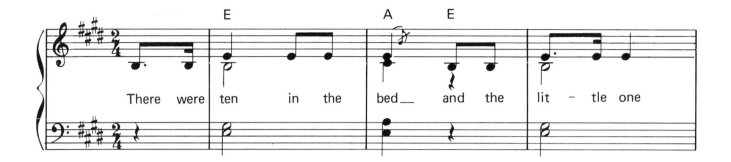

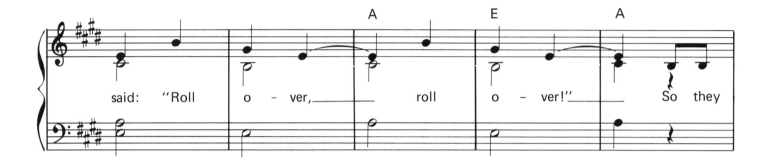

There were ten in the bed___ and the lit – tle one said: "Roll o – ver,___ roll o – ver!"___ So they

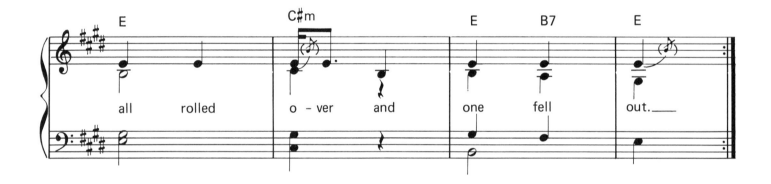

all rolled o – ver and one fell out.___

There were nine in the bed and the little one said, etc.

There were eight in the, etc.

There were seven in the, etc.

There were six in the, etc.

There were five in the, etc.

There were four in the, etc.

There were three in the, etc.

There were two in the, etc.

There was one in the bed and the little one said: "GOOD NIGHT!"

This Little Pig Went To Market

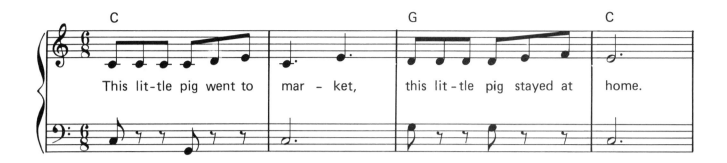

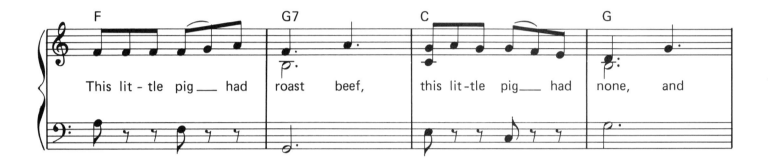

This lit-tle pig went to mar - ket, this lit-tle pig stayed at home.

This lit - tle pig — had roast beef, this lit-tle pig — had none, and

this lit - tle pig — cried we - we, we - we, we, all the way home.

This Old Man

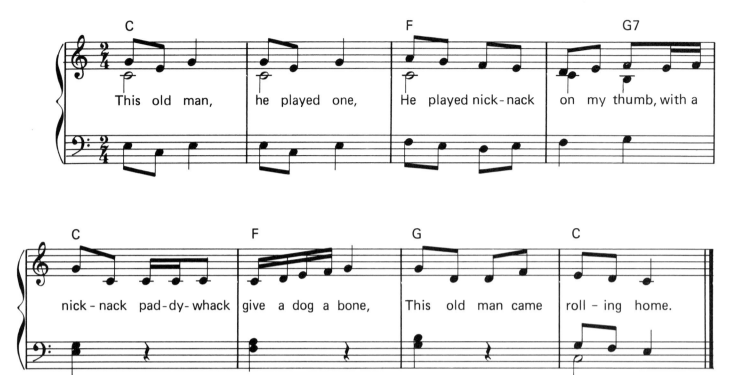

This old man, he played two . . . shoe, etc.

This old man, he played three . . . knee, etc.

Four . . . floor, etc.

Five . . . hive, etc.

Six . . . sticks, etc.

Seven . . . up in heaven, etc.

Eight . . . at my gate, etc.

Nine . . . on my spine, etc.

Ten . . . once again, etc.

Three Blind Mice

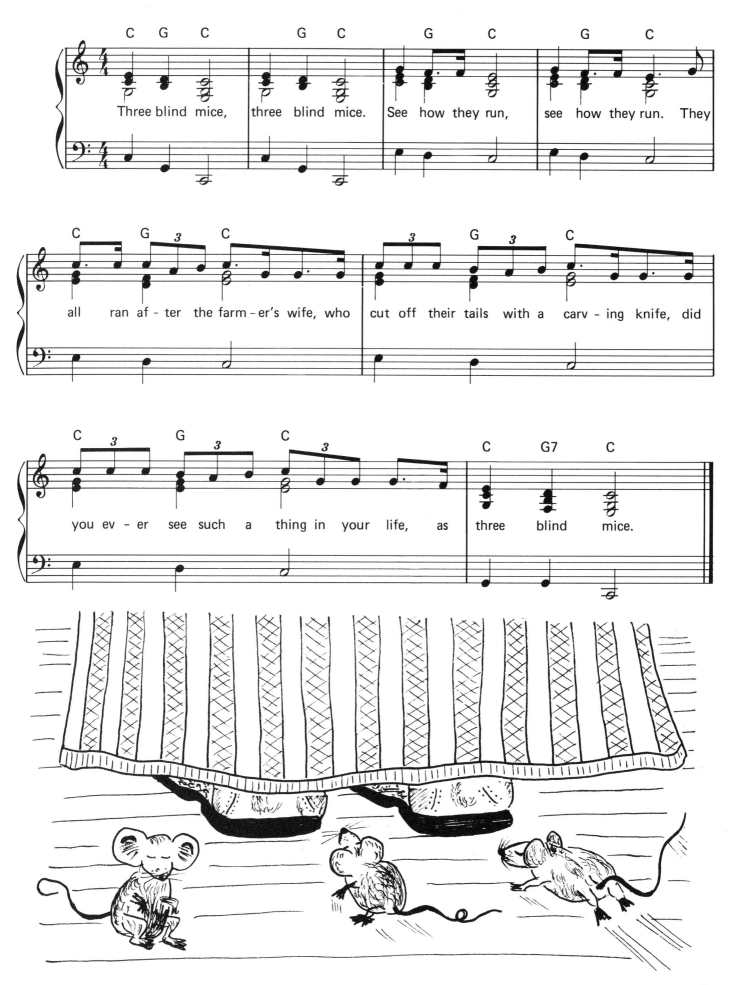

Three Little Kittens

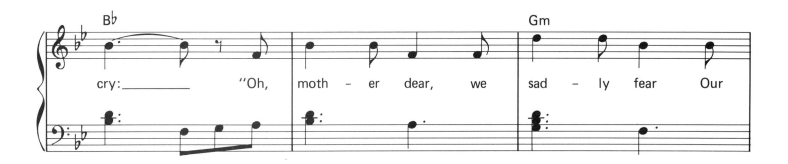

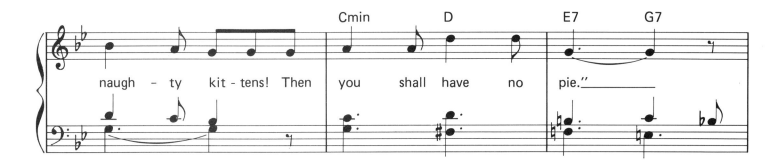

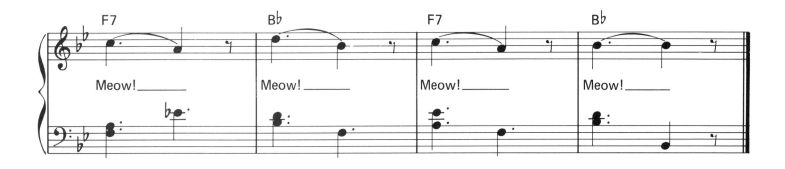

The three little kittens, they found their mittens,
And they began to cry:
"Oh, mother dear, see here, see here!
Our mittens we have found!"
"What! Found your mittens? You darling kittens!
Then you shall have some pie!"
"Meow! Meow! Meow! Meow!"

The three little kittens put on their mittens
And soon ate up the pie.
"Oh, mother dear, we greatly fear
Our mittens we have soiled."
"What! Soiled your mittens? You naughty kittens!"
Then they began to sigh,
"Meow! Meow! Meow! Meow!"

The three little kittens, they washed their mittens,
And hung them up to dry.
"Oh, mother dear, look here, look here!
Our mittens we have washed."
"What! Washed your mittens? You darling kittens!
But I smell a rat close by!
Hush! Hush! Hush! Hush!"

Two Little Dickey Birds

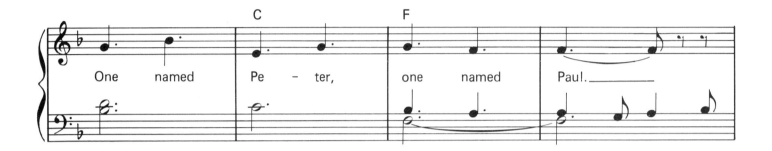

Two little dicky birds, sitting on a wall;
One named Peter, one named Paul.
Fly away, Peter! Fly away, Paul!
Come back, Peter! Come back, Paul!

Underneath The Spreading Chestnut Tree

Un - der - neath the spread-ing_____ chest - nut tree

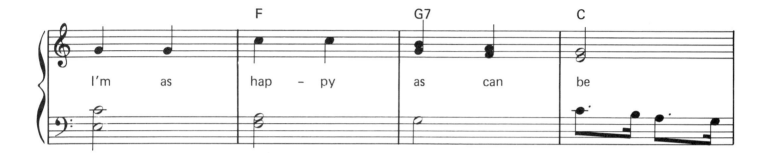

I'm as hap - py as can be

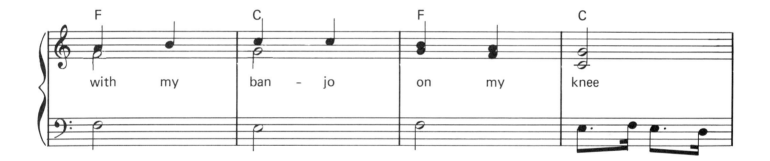

with my ban - jo on my knee

Un - der - neath the spread-ing_____ chest - nut tree.

Wee Willie Winkie

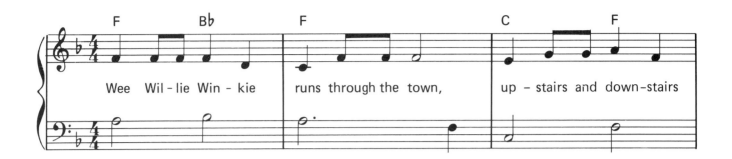

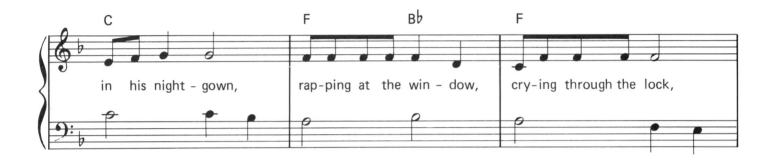

Wee Wil-lie Win-kie | runs through the town, | up-stairs and down-stairs

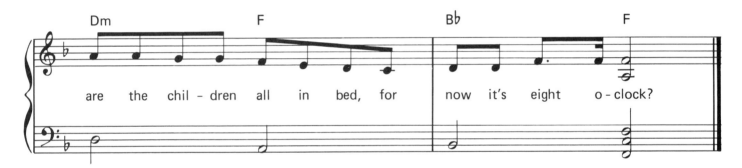

in his night-gown, | rap-ping at the win-dow, | cry-ing through the lock,

are the chil-dren all in bed, for | now it's eight o-clock?

Why Doesn't My Goose?